Hello Anna and Robin,

Thank you so much for helping my father (and me) with the rocks.

I thought I would give you a copy of my father's book (an obvious bestseller! ☺)

Anna (No. 19)

THE RED RIVER

by

PAUL WILLIAMS

Godrevy Press

First published in Great Britain by Godrevy Press, Cornwall

Dedication

To my late father John Kenneth Williams who always lived near the Red River and saw its many changes, particularly those of its flora and fauna.

Acknowledgments

Many people have advised me and suggested contacts and references. In particular I would like to acknowledge the help of Adrian Rodda who has given me a number of documents and references as well as reading a draft. The late Charles Thomas provided valuable verbal and published material. Sadly, this book was not published before his death. Brian and Elizabeth Jackson of Reskadinnick have provided invaluable help on the natural history of the valley as well as information on Stephen Mackenna and John Burley. Neil Williams and Kim Cooper of the Cornish Studies Library in Redruth have been very helpful in providing me with photographs. Joff Bullen has agreed to my use of the 1955 photograph of the tin works below Tuckingmill as well as giving me valuable information. This photograph is taken from the impressive Trounson-Bullen collection for which he holds copyright. Jem Southam has generously given me permission to use some of the excellent photographs from his book. From the Cornwall Archaeological Unit at Truro Bryn Tapper and Emma Trevarthen have provided aerial photographs and Jacky Nowakowski, senior archaeologist, has provided information of sites in the Red River valley.

Staff of the Royal Institution of Cornwall at Truro Museum have provided help in a number of ways. In particular Michael Harris and Sarah Lloyd-Durrant have helped with historic photographs of tin streaming and mining. Anna Tyacke has provided me with opinions and information. Angela Broome, the librarian has been very helpful with references. Sara Chambers has provided information on museum exhibits. Stephen Lay of Mineit Mining and Management Consultancy has also provided useful information. Allen Buckley, a major authority on the history of Cornish mining, has given me useful information on the mines discharging into the Red River. Tom Walker has provided me with information on his sedimentology research at the mouth of the valley. Stella Turk (who I have known for over 60 years) has provided historical information.

Help with the formatting has been provided by Imogen, Isobel and Anna Taylor, Katrina Hillman and Eleanor Oakley.

My thanks are due to them all.

Attribution of Photographs

Many of the photographs were taken by the author or his late father (JKW). Jem Southam has agreed to the use of a number of his excellent photographs from his book. He holds copyright. The Penlee House Gallery & Museum, Penzance have provided the photograph (taken by Gibsons of Penzance) of St Gothian's chapel. Copyright has expired. The photograph of the Red River at Godrevy, on the cover and in the text, was taken by Aerofilms. Copyright is held by Historic England. Copyright of the other photograph of the mouth of the river is held by Viewphotos. Many of the historic photographs were taken by the late Charles Woolf. Copyright is held by the Royal Institution of Cornwall (RIC). Copyright for most of the aerial photographs is held by the Historic Environment Record, Truro. (HER). That of Tolvaddon Valley Park in 2010 is held by Emma Trevarthen of the Cornish Archaeological Unit of Cornwall County Council at Truro. Copyright of a number of the photographs is held by the Cornish Studies Library at Redruth (CSL). A number of historic photographs are from the British Geological Survey (BGS). Copyright has expired. One of the historic photographs of the Red River valley below Tuckingmill is by courtesy of the Trounson-Bullen collection. Copyright is held by Mr. L.J. Bullen.

CONTENTS

INTRODUCTION 1

TOPOGRAPHY OF THE RED
RIVER VALLEY 8

THE RED RIVER IN PREHISTORY AND
THE DARK AND MIDDLE AGES 20

INDUSTRIALISATION 34

THE RED RIVER TODAY 57

THE NATURAL HISTORY OF
THE RED RIVER VALLEY 61

PEOPLE WHO HAVE LIVED IN
THE RED RIVER VALLEY 63

REFERENCES AND BIBLIOGRAPHY 73

INDEX 78

THE AUTHOR 83

INTRODUCTION

It is 1860. The Red River valley is a hive of activity and noise. Mines overlooking the valley are working full steam. The noise of the stamps crushing the ore is deafening. The beam engines driving the stamps along with the pumps and the cages are in constant use. Female bal maidens are breaking stones from the mines with hammers prior to them being transferred to the stamps. The ore from the stamps is being fed into mechanical machinery such as buddles to produce sand and slime which is fed with shovels into rag frames. The rag frames consist of long lines of sloping tables with wooden boxes above them. Into these flows water diverted from the Red River. The sandy mixture flows down the sloping tables to partially separate out the richer ore. At regular intervals, when the boxes become full, the water is automatically released as the wooden sides are lifted by the weight of water and then drop back. This adds to the noise. The waste material and water flows back into the Red River. The richer ore washes out into buckets. Further downstream streaming takes place to salvage more tin ore from the waste. The overall atmosphere in 1860 is one of noise and activity with over a thousand people employed.

This is the scene that would have assaulted the senses of any observer in the Red River valley for over a hundred years during the Industrial Revolution. It was then that the river acquired its red colour and present name having previously been known as the Connor River. The river is red because the water pumped out of the mines contained red iron ore. This water flows out from the mine adits that travel through the side of the valley and from there makes its way into the river. Until this time the valley had been a quiet, tranquil place, almost anonymous. It had been a place of slow change, the people there supporting themselves with small-scale industry and agriculture. The 18th and 19th century industrial activity transformed the narrow, attractive river meandering through Cornish countryside into what has been described as "One of the most modified rivers in the UK." (notice at entrance to Tuckingmill Country park). This book is an account of the Red River valley and its remarkable history.

The photographs below, taken in 1890 and 1904, record what it would have been like then, in contrast to now.

The Red River valley above Tuckingmill in 1890. (Foreground now covered by Camborne-Redruth relief road). (RIC)

Looking east across the valley from Dolcoath Mine in 1904 (taken by Bennetts of Camborne). (CSL)

The same location in 2015 is shown below.

Looking east across the Red River valley in 2015. (Author)

Rag frames below Tuckingmill. (CSL)

The photograph below taken in 1955, from below Tuckingmill, also shows what it would have been like then with little changed.

Valley north of Tuckingmill in 1955. (Trounson-Bullen collection)

However, since then much has changed as can be seen from the following photograph taken from the same location in 2012.

Valley north of Tuckingmill in 2012. (Author)

The red colour is shown dramatically in the photograph of 1978 shown on the cover of this book. When mining almost ceased (except for one mine, South Crofty) in the 1970s and tin streaming ceased in 1986 the river ceased to be red. But it is red again (or a dirty brown) as shown below.

Exit of adit at Roscroggan (2012). (Author)

The red colour now begins at Roscroggan where the Dolcoath adit discharges. The adit from South Crofty travels under the Red River to join the Dolcoath adit.

Red water joining the river at Roscroggan (2012). (Author)

Some remains of the industrial past are still present although sadly much was destroyed before it was considered worth conserving. However, in the lifetime of the author a lot still existed and is recorded in photographs in this book. It may seem paradoxical to decry the despoliation of the valley which occurred through mining and streaming yet also decry the destruction of the industrial heritage. But the original valley can never be recreated and the uniqueness of the industrial activity creates great interest. Some of the fauna and flora is returning and species have adapted to the waste environment although the waste has poisoned the ground and the river is largely sterile. Conservation projects have preserved some of the remains of the mining and streaming.

Long before the major industrial activity that occurred in the 18th and 19th centuries there is some evidence of alluvial tin extraction in earlier centuries. This is likely to have occurred in the Bronze

Age and through the Iron Age into Roman and Medieval times. Copper (which is needed with tin to form bronze) does not form alluvial deposits. It was probably obtained from lodes protruding through the granite very near the surface. Some of this history is recorded in this book.

At the present time it is possible to walk down most of the valley from the origin of the river above Bolenowe to the mouth at Godrevy although annoyingly the path is not totally complete (and designated footpaths have been blocked by land owners).

TOPOGRAPHY OF THE RED RIVER VALLEY

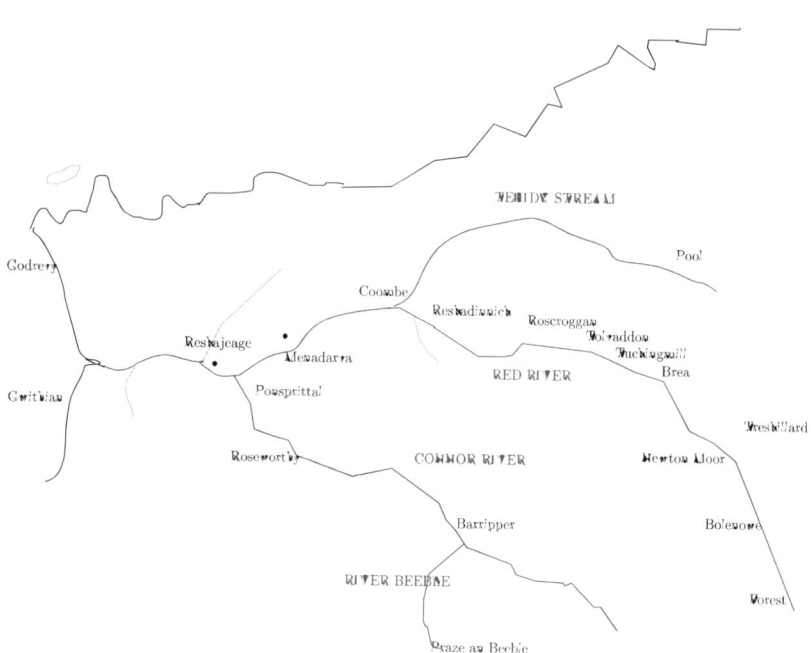

The Red River and its tributaries

The Red River rises in a series of springs in an area called 'Forest' just above the hamlet of Bolenowe. It is near the watershed in this part of Cornwall. The Hayle River, which flows out further west, rises nearby as does the Cober River which flows out through Helston into Loe Pool on the south coast.

The Red River rises at a height of about 184 metres and flows for about 7 miles to reach the north coast between Godrevy and Gwithian. It flows as a small unpolluted stream through the hamlets of Bolenowe and Newton Moor to the village of Brea.

Red River stream above Bolenowe (2012). (Author)

Source of the Red River above Bolenowe (2012). (Author)

Bolenowe (1980s). (Jem Southam)

Brea from gorge (Brea Adit). (2012) (Author)

Settling beds at Brea (2012). (Author)

It is here, at Brea, that the tin streaming began and remains can still be seen.

The river was canalised for much of the next stretch with concrete walls to control its course. They can still be seen. Then it flows into Tuckingmill where there were once extensive tin streaming works in what is now the Tuckingmill Valley Park and at Tolvaddon (some since covered by the Camborne-Redruth bypass). Until the 1980's the arsenic flues and stacks for burning off the impurities from the tin ore were very prominent in this area.

Canalised Red River at Tolvaddon (1960s) (now covered by bypass). (Author)

From here on the river grows wider although it remains a stream all the way to the coast. Extensive tin streaming continued down the valley past Tolvaddon to Roscroggan. At Roscroggan the river once again becomes red (2015) as an adit enters from modern mining activity. Then further on at Reskadinnick a tiny tributary from Camborne joins. This flows past the old Rosewarne Manor and past Reskadinnick House. Just after the remains of mineral processing at Kieve Mill, at Coombe, the Tehidy tributary joins. This flows from Pool, sometimes underground, past old tin streaming works and is diverted into the lake in Tehidy Park. This ornamental lake was created by the Basset family in front of their (now largely demolished) mansion. Through the woods at Tehidy it passes over cascades and eventually joins the Red River at Coombe.

Old tin streaming works on Tehidy stream tributary (1960s) (now flattened). (Author)

Beyond this the Red River passes Bell Lake which was once much larger before being half-clogged with reeds. It probably powered a water mill.

Bell Lake (2012). (Author)

It then makes its way through the hamlet of Menadarva with its medieval farmstead and ancient bridge.

Bridge at Menadarva (2012). (Author)

A little further on, at Ponsprittal, the Connor River joins. This is the largest tributary and originates near Boswyn, above the recently re-erected Carwynnen Quoit. The Connor river flows down into the lake below the former (now demolished) Pendarves Manor. From there it flows past Barripper into Roseworthy (where there were also mineral workings) to join the Red River a little below Menadarva. The Connor river also has the tiny River Beeble (giving its name to Praze-an-Beeble) as a tributary. This joins at Barripper.

Just below the join with the Connor River there are ancient woods of willow in the boggy ground. The river then opens out into a wider valley past the former water mill at Reskajeage. Here the river has been diverted and canalised within high hedges (occasionally breached) since it flows at, or above, the level of the surrounding land. At Reskajeage another tiny stream, which originates in the valley behind Hell's Mouth, joins and then, a bit further on, a tiny stream from Gwithian Village also joins.

Join of Red River with Connor river (1980s). (Jem Southam)

It has been suggested that the valley was tidal up to Reskajeage and possibly beyond until silted by mining waste and blown sand. This looks very plausible given the flat plain and its discontinuity with the slope of the surrounding ground (see the photographs). However, very surprisingly, recent research based on the sinking of bore holes has suggested otherwise (see references). It is suggested that there was no tidal inlet north of the present river. South of the river the research suggests the tidal inlet would have come little further than just beyond the present Gwithian Bridge. The height of the river compared with the surrounding land added credence to the possibility of an inlet. The land is prevented from flooding on high tides by banks near the mouth. In the past the river is thought to have flowed further to the south as well as meandering and flowing out west of the current exit.

Valley nearing Gwithian (2012). (Author)

Flood plane looking towards Godrevy and St. Ives Bay (2015). (Author)

The last section of the Red River (2014). (Author)

Mining waste has also been carried into the sea from the river for centuries. Up until the 1980s the sea was red near the mouth. Grey tin waste still covers the beach. Processing of the sand to try to extract tin continued after mining almost ceased as did streaming.

A little further on the river joins the sea. Although still 'dirty' it has been diluted to a dull grey colour (2015) compared with the vivid red apparent in 1978 seen in the photograph on the cover of this book.

Near mouth of Red River at Reskajeage (2011). (HER)

From the map it can be seen that the basin of the Red River encompasses much of the former mining area of Camborne and Redruth (once the major mineral extraction area of the world).

Mouth of the Red River in the 1970s. (Viewphotos)

Even before the extensive industrial activity of the 18th and 19th centuries the river valley saw much activity. There were settlements along the sides of the valley through all prehistoric periods and probably alluvial tin extraction as well.

Godrevy is enhanced by Godrevy Island with its lighthouse (built in 1859). This is the lighthouse which inspired the famous novel 'To the Lighthouse' by Virginia Woolf. The scene has inspired many artists. The book 'Godrevy Light' by Charles Thomas and Jessica Mann contains many attractive pictures.

Godrevy Island. (Author)

THE RED RIVER IN PREHISTORY AND THE DARK AND MIDDLE AGES

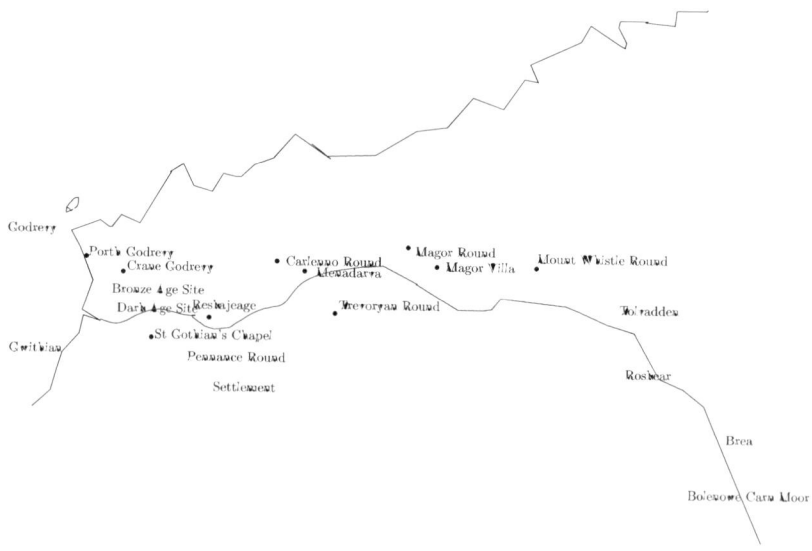

Red River sites in Prehistory and the Dark and Middle Ages.

Long before the industrialisation of the 18th and 19th centuries, which so transformed the valley and the river, the Red River (not red) was the scene of much activity. Although it is convenient to categorise habitation into different periods (Stone Age, Bronze Age, Iron Age etc.) habitation was mainly continuous and periods merged into each other.

Beginning just above the source there is a dilapidated Bronze Age cairn known as 'Hangman's Barrow' (the Bronze Age is taken as roughly 2500BC to 800BC). Fairly close to this, just above the Red River, on the hill to the west (Bolenowe Carn Moor) are the remains of a settlement.

This looks like a Courtyard Village, of the sort found in West Penwith (eg Chysauster, Carn Euny, Porthmeor and Mulfra). If so this would have been Iron Age/Romano-British (The Iron Age was roughly 800BC to 43AD and the Roman occupation of Britain 43AD to 410AD) and might have been occupied up to the 3rd century AD. The area south and west (some of the highest land in the area, up to Crowan Beacon) also had settlements and stone circles. It is likely that the people in these settlements streamed the Red River for alluvial tin. It is interesting to note that on the side of the hill from Bolenowe Carn Moor down to Bolenowe in the garden of 'Home Farm' (once occupied by ancestors of the author) there is a cave known as 'The Wink'.

The Wink at Bolenowe

There are a number of such caves known as 'hulls' in the area. They were thought to have been built in the 18th or 19th centuries, although some are thought to be much earlier. They were used for storing dairy and agricultural goods at uniform temperatures and possibly also smuggled goods brought up from Gwithian. In many ways they are similar to the fougous which neighbour the courtyard villages of West Penwith.

It is interesting to note that the Roman historian Tacitus describes the Germans hollowing out underground caves, covering them with manure and using them as store houses and refuges from winter frosts. He also claimed that they hid in their bolt holes to escape detection from raiders, which was one function of the souterrains of Gaul and early medieval Ireland. Contemporary evidence supports the view that fougous were used for food storage.

Further down, at Brea on the east bank, it was reported that there was an Iron Age 'camp'. No trace seems visible now, almost certainly destroyed by mining activity. Moving down the river further prehistoric remains would also have been destroyed by mining and tin streaming activity although, ever visible, the hill of Carn Brea, just to the east, was a major Neolithic site (the Neolithic period is taken as 4000BC to 2500BC).

Down the Red River valley from upper reaches with Carn Brea on the right (2012). (Author)

At Tuckingmill a logboat (possibly Bronze Age) was found in 1870 under the gasworks beside the then A30 road. Together with it was a beautiful greenstone adze.

Replica logboat in National Maritime museum at Falmouth (2012). (Author)

Adze found with logboat at Tuckingmill. (Author)

No trace remains of the logboat although it was probably similar to the modern replica logboat shown in the National Maritime Museum at Falmouth. The adze would have been used for carving the boat out from the log. It is now in Helston museum.

The discovery of the logboat was suggested as evidence that the Red River was navigable from the sea at Godrevy up to Tuckingmill before it became silted with mine waste. This seems unlikely given the gradient. One possible explanation is that it was used as a 'ferry' across the then wider and deeper river. The modern trunk road could have followed the route of an ancient trackway through Cornwall with a need to take the ferry at what is now Tuckingmill. A similar logboat was found at the mouth of the Newlyn River.

A little below Tuckingmill, on the west of the valley, is Roskear. No archaeological remains are extant but 'Roskear' means 'defended camp' which suggests an Iron Age encampment/settlement. In the valley below and above, on the opposite side, is Tolvaddon, again the former site of much industrial activity. In the early 1900s the archaeologist Thurstan Peter excavated an encampment slightly further up the valley. A bronze rapier, illustrated below and now in Truro Museum, was found together with a similarly dated palstave. They are thought to date from the middle Bronze Age. In fact, it is possible that many of the rounds found along the valley date from the Bronze Age but continued throughout the Iron Age.

Bronze rapier found in 1909 near Tolvaddon. (Author)

The intense industrial activity continued down to Roscroggan and would have destroyed any other prehistoric remains. However above Roscroggan, to the north, lies the site of Mount Whistle Round.

Mount Whistle Round (in middle of picture): (a Roman site?) (1992). (HER)

Nothing is visible on the ground but it is clearly visible in the aerial photograph, shown above. It is an almost square 'round' and is also shown on old maps. Ploughing must have destroyed the old banks and any internal structures. Its square shape could be taken to suggest it was Roman (the Roman Occupation was AD43 to AD410). The lower hedge has clearly been bent to accommodate the encampment (but why has the lower hedge in the next field below been bent?)

About a third of a mile west, still on the north side of the valley, the only Roman villa west of Exeter was found. Its proximity to Mount Whistle Round seems more than a coincidence. It was excavated in 1931. Many artefacts, including Roman coins, were found. They are all now in Truro Museum. Known as Magor (meaning 'ruined walls') Villa it lies close to Magor Farm. It is now covered up but the remains are shown in the photographs below.

Magor Roman Villa, looking west in 1931. (CSL)

Magor Roman Villa, looking east 1931. (CSL)

It is thought that the villa is 'Romano-Cornish' and might have been constructed by a Cornishman (a member of the Dumnonii tribe) who returned after seeing villas in other parts of the country. Apparently its quality is inferior to most other villas. It was occupied in the second half of the second century AD. Very close to the site of the villa, to the north-west, was another round (Magor Round), now demolished, but visible in aerial photos. This is on the spur of land between the join of the Tehidy stream with the Red River. The closeness of these last three sites to each other seems significant.

Going down the river beyond Menadarva, on the north bank of the river, there is another round at Carlenno. The banks are now almost gone and the ditches very shallow but it shows up in the aerial photograph below.

Remains of Carlenno Round (in middle of picture) (2011). (HER)

The site of yet another round was just to the west of Reskajeage farm. Others have been found on the north side of the river. There was one below the remains of Crane Godrevy on the top of the Godrevy headland. There are two more (at least) on the south side of the river at Trevoryan, opposite Menadarva, and a bit further up the valley, at Pennance near Nanterrow. Both these two have been ploughed out but their outlines are visible from aerial photographs. In the latter case the hedge of the field follows the outline of the round. At Garrack on the spur of land opposite Reskajeage it is reported that there was a medieval village. The site looks reminiscent of a round in the photograph below.

Possible site of a round at Garrack (2012). (Author)

It is now thought that these sites were more likely to have been habitable enclosures for people and livestock, rather than defensive forts. Their prevalence along the Red River valley seems significant. Unfortunately, many have been demolished by agricultural work within less than the last hundred years and those that remain have been reduced to shallow banks and ditches. Did the inhabitants obtain tin from the alluvial deposits in the river? Did they cooperate and trade with the Romans? The fact that many rounds are beside 'modern' (although still old) farms suggests continuous farming and habitation of these sites through time. The population of the Red River valley, during the Iron Age, could have been considerable.

The area near the mouth of the river has produced much prehistoric information both before and after the Iron Age. Near the headland, to the north of the river (Porth Godrevy), extensive Mesolithic (8000BC to 4000BC) sites and remains were found (eg flints). These must have been made from beach pebbles as no natural flint occurs here. A Bronze Age site (2500BC to 800BC) was discovered and excavated closer to the river on its north side, just below the large hill before the headland. It is thought that this site was inhabited for 900 years. There have been a number of Roman remains found in the area: coins from Gwithian Beach (as well as Magor Villa) and two artefacts thought to have come from the Red River between Godrevy and Menadarva as well as Roman pottery. At Porth Godrevy there was a small Roman site and a Roman (?) broach was found. Even if the Romans did not have a major presence west of Exeter they must have traded and interacted with the inhabitants of the Red River valley. When the Romans left in 410 AD Briton entered into the Dark Ages (the period up to 1066). Many prefer to call this era the post-Roman period. In Cornwall little probably changed immediately although the coming of Christianity to Cornwall was highly significant and there are many remains of the early Christian period (stone crosses, small churches etc.).

Close to the river on the north bank near the mouth lies a small bank/peninsula on which were found Dark Age workshops. This is evidence of small-scale industry that preceded the larger-scale industry of the 18th and 19th century.

This area is shown in the photograph below, looking up the river.

Dark Age site (with Bronze Age site in foreground) (2012). (Author)

It should be remembered that Marram grass was planted on the dunes only just over 200 years ago to stabilise the sand. Prior to that the landscape would largely have consisted of shifting sands. The buildings which were excavated on the post-Roman site appeared to involve smelting and metalwork as well as leather work and pottery. They were occupied from the latter part of the 5th century until the 8th century. Middens were found containing large numbers of mussel shells. The Ceres rock off Gwithian Beach, only exposed at low tide, provides a plentiful source of large mussels for local people today. It seems very likely that this was also the case in the past. The fact that the rock is submerged for most of the day creates an ideal environment for the mussels.

At Gwithian/Godrevy, St. Gothians's Chapel lies buried under the sand, on slightly raised ground, near the tributary from Gwithian. It was seen in the 19th century, when the photograph below was taken, before being buried by blown sand.

St Gothian's Chapel (1880). (Penlee Museum and Gallery)

One of the walls was exposed again in 2001. St. Gothian was by legend an Irish saint. Many saints came to Cornwall to spread Christianity from both Ireland and Wales. St Gothian is the origin of the name 'Gwithian'. The chapel was probably built in the 6th century (contemporary with the Dark Ages site).

An early Christian chapel is also recorded at Menadarva (the Chapel of St Derwa giving rise to the name 'Menadarva'). The very attractive farm is recorded as 17th and 18th century but outbuildings (with a mullioned window) could be much earlier.

Menadarva Farm House (2015). (Author)

Mullioned Window at Menadarva (2015). (Author)

The occupation of the valley seems to have had a smooth transition into the Middle Ages. Other farms/manors, in the lower reaches of the valley, appear to have had medieval origins. Outbuildings at Reskajeage and Gwealavellan appear to be medieval.

Medieval (?) outbuildings at Reskajeage Farm (2015). (Author)

There are reported to be signs of medieval settlements /farmsteads close by at Tolgarrack and at Garrack (on the opposite side of the river). In Gwithian village there was the medieval manor of Connerton, recorded in the Domesday Book. It is thought that this was part of a now buried village. On this site there is a 16th century pound, presumably for holding impounded livestock. This is beside the present day Gwithian Church which dates from the 13th century. On the hill on the north side of the river, overlooking some of the prehistoric sites, are the remains of the medieval sub-manor of Crane Godrevy. This was built on part of the Iron Age round. It dates from the 14th century.

Throughout the Middle Ages, and before, it seems likely that streaming for alluvial tin was taking place. Bore holes sunk near

Remains of the medieval sub-manor of Crane Godrevy (1957). (Author)

the mouth of the river suggests there was no large scale mining further up the valley before about 1050. However, smaller shafts were almost certainly sunk much earlier. Tin was probably smelted in prehistoric and Dark Age times using charcoal harvested from woods. From the early 14th century blowing houses were used where the necessary heat was generated by means of bellows, possibly powered by water wheels. From the 18th century onwards reverberatory furnaces were used. These required coal which needed to be imported from South Wales. The name 'Tuckingmill' means 'fulling mill' and is mentioned in 1250. Fulling was the process of soaking and beating woollen cloth prior to its use.

On Norden's map of Cornwall, surveyed in 1584, the only farmsteads marked on the sides of the valley are Menadarva and Treswithian (back somewhat from the river).

INDUSTRIALISATION

Although there is evidence that some underground mining took place earlier and the alluvial extraction of tin had certainly been pursued for centuries, it was in the 18th century that the dramatic industrialisation took place. Tin and copper mines were dug on both sides of the Red River valley. Their discharge of water and waste into the river transformed it. Alluvial tin extraction now became a major activity. Since photography was only invented in 1839 there are no earlier photographs of the valley or the mines. Some of the mines along the sides of the Red River valley, in the 19th century, are shown below. There were many more, mostly marginal.

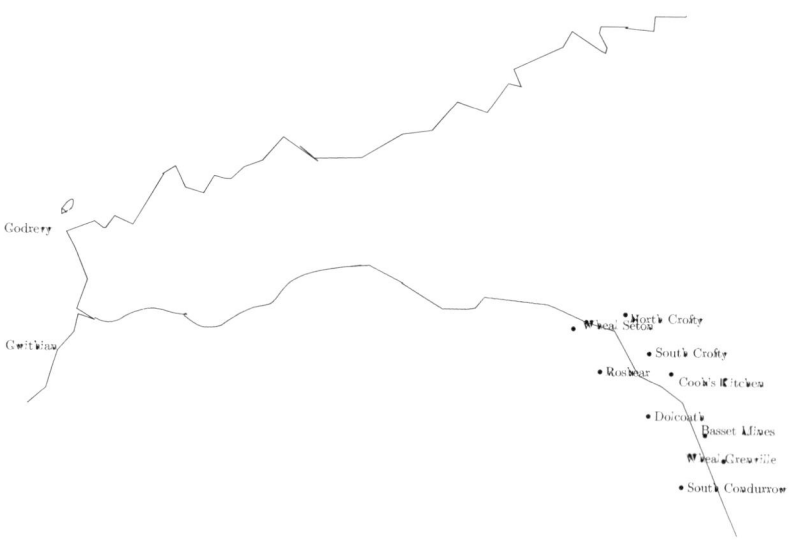

Some major mines in the Red River valley in the 19th and early 20th century.

A picture of the valley above Tuckingmill and some of the mines on the east bank is shown in the Introduction. Many of the mines and the mineral rights were held by the Basset family from Tehidy, who had lived there since the Norman Conquest. They became one of the richest families in Britain as a result of mining.

When mining was at its peak, in the 19th and early 20th century, there were mines on the sides of the Red River valley at Carn Brea, TinCroft, Cook's Kitchen, South Crofty, North Crofty, Dolcoath, and West Seton all pouring water out from their lower levels into the Red River through adits. This was accomplished through the great advances in steam engines, with compressors, driving beam engines to lift water up to the level of the adits. Other beam engines drove the stamps for crushing the ore along with the kibbles which carried the ore to the surface and the cages for transporting miners up and down the shafts (some shafts were over 3000 feet deep). The enormous beam engines were accommodated in the high mine buildings whose remains still litter the landscape, such as those shown below.

Wheal Grenville on west side of the Red River (1992). (JKW)

In addition, ore was transported by mineral trains to the Red River, for processing, from East Pool and Agar mines, about a mile away. The Red River, augmented by the water from the mines, played a major part in the treatment (dressing) of the ore coming out of the mines.

Some stamps were driven by water wheels powered by diversions of the Red River through leats.

Water wheel at Tuckingmill (c1930). (CSL)

Convex buddles at Brea Adit (2012). (Author)

After the ore had been broken up by bal maidens, to separate out the richer content, it was crushed by the stamps into a coarse sand. Water was diverted from the Red River to wash this sand over buddles where the richer tin-bearing sand was separated out through gravity. Other means were also used. Vibrating sloping (James) tables were used to wash the water over them and separate out the tin.

A Vibrating (James) table. (Author)

Rag frames (pictured in the Introduction) performed a similar purpose. The water which had flowed through the buddles, the rag frames and vibrating tables still contained (less concentrated) tin ore. It went back into the Red River but it was still worth trying to extract further tin. As well as sometimes being passed over similar dressing devices again it was also fed slowly into settling beds where the heavier tin-bearing sand settled out. The beds were long channels between stone or concrete built walls, such as those shown at Brea in section 2.

An adjustable sluice, to control the rate of flow into these beds at Brea, is shown below.

Adjustable sluice, at Brea, for controlling flow through the settling bed (2012). (Author)

Other settling beds are shown further (on the next page) down the river above Tuckingmill.

The Red River and settling beds at Tuckingmill (1980s). (Jem Southam)

The same area is shown below in 2012.

Red River above Tuckingmill (2012). (Author)

Different families and businesses set up tin streams further down the valley to reprocess the waste from earlier processing. In 1884 there were 23 tin stream organisations in the Red River valley. The last works, Tolgarrick Tin at Tolvaddon, closed in 1986. All the time this waste was red from the (unusable) iron ore in it. The rich, red colour of the river can be seen in the photo below, taken in the 1970s.

The Red River in the 1970s. (Jem Southam)

The total effect of the dressing machinery (now largely destroyed) and the successive tin streaming works down the valley was to transform it totally. This was before the days of conservation movements. Another major transformation of the environment resulted from the need to remove the arsenic impurity from the dressed ore before smelting. This was achieved by roasting the ore in calciners and letting out the toxic smoke through high stacks. Water from the Red River was used to quench the roasted ore.

Remains of calciner beside the river at Tolvaddon (2012). (Author)

The condensed arsenic was scraped off the sides and roofs of flues, such as those shown on the next page at Tolvaddon in the 1960s. The arsenic was exported to be used as a pesticide. It was also used in dyes and paints and as a medicine. The author remembers his grandmother saying that the potatoes grown in the fields around arsenic stacks were better than those from elsewhere. He also remembers the tale of a Devon farmer who bought a herd of cows that grazed on fields near arsenic stacks and were in very good condition. However, once they had been moved to Devon they quickly lost condition much to the displeasure of the purchasing farmer.

Arsenic flues at Tolvaddon (1960s). (RIC)

Looking south with Tolvaddon stacks on the left. (RIC)

The high stacks were a major feature of the valley. Two of them were a landmark at the top of the hill at Tolvaddon. They are shown in the photograph below taken in the 1960s. They can be seen in the background of a number of the other photographs. Later they were demolished to make way for the bypass.

Stacks at Tolvaddon in the 1960s. (Author)

A much older photograph (late 19th or early 20th century) is shown below.

Stacks at Tolvaddon. (RIC)

Further on at Tolvaddon there were tin streams shown in the photograph in section 2 and those below.

Red river channel and old workings at Tolvaddon (2012). (Author)

The same location in the 1900s. (RIC)

Looking north from Tolvaddon towards West Seton (1999). (JKW)

From a similar location in the 1960s with remains of arsenic flues. (RIC)

Buddles at West Seton. (RIC)

Going further down the valley there were more works at Roscroggan, now largely destroyed. Further down still were the Reskadinnick tin streams. The large bank of rag frames is shown below. In the background is a corn mill and Canadian pine trees planted in the early 1900s.

Rag frames at Reskadinnick (1930). (BGS)

Reskadinnick tin streams looking east. (BGS)

The river below Reskadinnick in 2012 is shown below.

The Red River below Reskadinnick in 2012. (Author)

The next stream works were at Kieve Mill. This was near the site of the current sewage/water treatment works and the beginning of the tunnel which discharges treated sewage from west Cornwall out into the sea beyond Godrevy.

A photograph of the stream works in 1904 is shown below.

Tin streaming works at Kieve Mill (1904). (BGS)

The same location in 2012. (Author)

Another picture of the rag frames at Kieve Mill, taken in 1904 is shown below.

Rag frames at Kieve Mill (1904). (BGS)

The same, rather forlorn, location in 2012. (Author)

Settling beds with adjustable sluices, at Kieve Mill, in 1904. (BGS)

The same location in 2012, with remains of a sluice just visible. (Author)

Just downstream from Kieve Mill the Tehidy stream joins at Coombe. A picture of the river (still red) in 2012 under the road bridge at Coombe is given below.

The Red River at Coombe (2012). (Author)

The Red River below Coombe (1904). (BGS)

The same (overgrown) location in 2012. (Author)

Just after Coombe is the beautiful and peaceful Bell Lake. The name is a derivation of 'Combellack'. It is thought that once it was the site of a lake which powered a water mill. Originally it would have been much larger as can be seen from the aerial photograph below with both ends visible. The middle is choked with reeds. It is of much interest to naturalists.

Bell Lake (2006). (HER)

The river flows on past Menadarva. In places the banks have been stabilised by faggots as shown in the picture below.

Faggots edging the bank of the river near Menadarva (2014). (Author)

It can also be seen that the red in the river is becoming diluted as it approaches the flood plane near Gwithian.

Finally, the dramatic effects of the mining and streaming activity at the outlet at Godrevy is shown on the photograph below taken in 1978.

Outlet of the Red River at Godrevy in 1978. Historic England Archive (Aerofilms)

The result of the pollution from the Red River was to deposit tin bearing sand on the beach and in the bay. A number of attempts have been made to recover and process this. Between the 19th century and World War II processing of sand from the beach took place. The waves and tides sometimes had the effect of concentrating tin bearing sand in particular areas. The Red River was diverted to drive a water wheel and also to aid the processing of the sand so as to concentrate the tin in it. An aqueduct to carry water was also built and an overhead ropeway was used to transport sand across the beach to the works. Arsenic was burnt off using calciners with their associated stacks. Despite considerable investment the enterprise seems to have met with limited commercial success and closed in 1940.

Beach sand was also removed in large quantities and transported inland in lorries to be used for agriculture and construction (eg rebuilding Plymouth after the war).

In the 1960s an attempt was made to extract tin bearing sand from the sea bed using a dredger. Sand was sucked up and put through concentrating machinery. However, the yields were such as to make the transition from prospecting to commercial extraction non-viable.

THE RED RIVER TODAY

Since the last tin streaming closed in 1986 and South Crofty closed in 1998 (but temporarily reopened in 2003) the valley has changed again. Vegetation has returned to some areas but the scars of industrialisation remain. A major change was caused by the Camborne-Redruth bypass which was built in 1975. This goes over the valley at Tolvaddon. Stacks were taken down to accommodate it. No provision was made for a path or cycle track through the valley and under the bypass. Walkers and cyclists have to climb up and cross the bypass or walk along the road past Roskear Croft. Even at Roskear Croft, and in the valley below, the path has been closed. An aerial view of the bypass and valley adjacent to it is shown below.

Tuckingmill Valley Park with the bypass to the north (2010). (HER)

Camborne-Redruth bypass looking east and passing over the Red River valley (2012). (Author)

A picture of the bypass in relation to some old mine workings at Tolvaddon is shown below.

Looking south over the bypass towards South Crofty (1999). (JKW)

Between Tuckingmill and the bypass the Tuckingmill Valley Park has been created. This preserves what remains of the industrial past with some collapsed arsenic flues and chimneys (see photographs in section 3) and capped shafts and adits. Much information is given on signs. In addition, pools have been created in order to encourage flora and fauna to return.

It is possible to walk down some stretches of the valley. Near the source, above Bolenowe, one can follow a road on the west of the river through Bolenowe, Newton Moor and Brea to Tuckingmill. Then the rural path can be followed through Tuckingmill Valley Park. At the northern end of the Park one has to climb up to the road on the east and follow this through the modern housing estate at Tolvaddon. It is frustrating to look down into the valley and see what used to be paths on either side of the river now blocked by private householders. A small path then leaves the road and skirts the top of the valley to come out halfway down Roscroggan Hill. The road has to be followed crossing the bridge over the river at the bottom of the hill (and missing out some of the old Roscroggan tin streaming works). One can take a short lane from the south to the north of the river past Red River Cottage (in the garden of which is the exit from the adit now discharging red into the river) before joining a path beside the river on the north bank.

One then passes ponds created since the end of streaming. The reclamation of this stretch is shown on the following page. From here there is the longest stretch of uninterrupted path going from Roscroggan past Reskadinnick, Kieve Mill, Coombe (where the Tehidy stream joins), Bell Lake and Menadarva. This is part of the Red River Valley Nature Reserve. The short part of the path below Menadarva is very interesting with its ancient scrub woodland. Unfortunately, it soon comes to an end just past Ponsprittal (where the Conner river joins). Now the canalised river goes through very boggy private land. No further open path remains. One has to backtrack and go to Gwithian Bridge to walk the last small stretch of the river to its mouth. At one time larger sections of the river valley would have been traversable.

Some industrialisation (as discussed in the Introduction) is

Reclamation work at Roscroggan (1993). (JKW)

proposed using the former South Crofty mine. It has been suggested that the rare earth metal indium be mined along with tin and zinc. Indium is a rare earth mineral used in the manufacture of touch-screen computers. The waste (coming out of the adit at Roscroggan) is again colouring the river from there onwards.

THE NATURAL HISTORY OF THE RED RIVER VALLEY

This is a brief summary of the major aspects of the natural history of the regenerating Red River valley. A more comprehensive account with a full list of species of both animals and plants can be found in the work of Brian and Elizabeth Jackson referenced.

The poisoning of both the Red River and the surrounding corridor as well as around the neighbouring mines has had a dramatic effect on the fauna and flora as well as the landscape. Although it is nearly a century since many of the mines and tin streams ceased a lot of the land is still barren. The river is still sterile in places, particularly from where the new discharge enters the river at Roscroggan. However, new species have emerged in many areas to counter the hostile terrain. They are sometimes unique to the area and make the valley a very interesting environment. In some locations, notably Tuckingmill Valley Park and around some former mines, contaminated soil has been removed to be replaced by fresh soil. Into this different plants, shrubs and trees have been introduced. This is not without controversy, it being argued that the immediate post-mining and streaming environment should be preserved in view of its uniqueness and the rare species that emerge from it. Some think the area around mines and streaming works should not be converted to gardens which would look artificial.

The ponds created in the Tuckingmill Valley Park and at Roscroggan as well as the much older Bell Lake are home to an abundance of wildlife. Sticklebacks, minnows, frogs, toads, eels and newts are present. The stretch of the valley from Roscroggan to Menadarva is a nature reserve.

Foxes and badgers live in the valley. In the spring the gorse comes out. Its yellow flowers are a major feature of the valley, growing on the old waste tips for much of the rest of the year. In the summer butterflies and dragonflies hatching from the ponds and lake appear. One of the country's rarest is the blue-tailed damselfly. Another rare species is the small red damselfly. The pyramid orchid also comes out in the summer. Heather appears in the autumn. A large variety of birds now inhabit and breed in the valley.

Once again the valley is a tranquil yet stimulating and unique place for nature lovers.

PEOPLE WHO HAVE LIVED IN THE RED RIVER VALLEY

This is a short account of some notable people who have lived in the Red River valley. Of course, many other estimable people have lived there as well.

The Cornish Poet **John Harris** (1820-1884) was born and lived at Bolenowe.

At the age of 12 he was sent to work at Dolcoath mine where he was employed for 20 years. During this time, he wrote his poems using blackberry juice on scraps of cardboard. They are beautiful poems capturing the atmosphere of the area and the times. A John Harris Society has been formed to celebrate his work. His poems have been reproduced in a number of books. The full set is given in one of the references.

We reproduce one, 'The Mine' here.

A mine spread out its vast machinery.
Here engines with their huts and smoky stacks,
Cranks, wheels, and rods, boilers and hissing steam,
Pressed up the water from the depths below.
Here fire-whims ran till almost out of breath,
And chains cried sharply, strained with fiery force.
Here blacksmiths hammered by the sooty forge,
And there a crusher crashed the copper ore.
Here girls were cobbing under roofs of straw,
And there were giggers at the oaken hutch.
Here a man-engine glided up and down,
A blessing and a boon to mining men:
And near the spot, where many years before,
Turned round and round the rude old water wheel,
A huge fire-stamps was working evermore,
And slimy boys were swarming at the trunks.
The noisy lander by the trap-door bawled
With pincers in his hand; and troops of maids
With heavy hammers brake the mineral stones.
The cart-man cried, and shook his broken whip;
And on the steps of the account-house stood
The active agent, with his eye on all.

Below were caverns grim with greedy gloom,
And levels drunk with darkness; chambers huge
Where Fear sat silent, and the mineral-sprite

For ever chanted his bewitching song;
Shafts deep and dreadful, looking darkest things
And seeming almost running down to doom;
Rock under foot, rock standing on each side;
Rock cold and gloomy, frowning overhead;
Before; behind, at every angle, rock.
Here blazed a vein of precious copper ore,
Where lean men laboured with a zeal for fame,
With face and hands and vesture black as night,
And down their sides the perspiration ran
In steaming eddies, sickening to behold.
But they complained not, digging day and night,
And morn and eve, with lays upon their lips.
Here yawned a tin-cell like a cliff of crags,
Here Danger lurked among the groaning rocks,
And oftimes moaned in darkness. All the air
Was black with sulphur and burning up the blood.
A nameless mystery seemed to fill the void,
And wings all pitchy flapped among the flints,
And eyes that saw not sparkled min the spars.
Yet here men worked, on stages hung in ropes,
With drills and hammers blasting the rude earth,
Which fell with such a crash that he who heard
Cried, "Jesu, save the miner!" Here were the ends
Cut through hard marble by the miners' skill,
And winzes, stopes and rizes: pitches here,
Where worked the heroic, princely tributer,
This month for nothing, next for fifty pounds.

Here lodes ran wide, and there so very small
That scarce a pick-point could be pressed between;
Here making walls as smooth as polished steel,
And there as craggy as a rended hill.

And out of sparry vagues the water oozed,
Staining the rock with mineral, so that oft
It led the labourer to a house of gems.
Across the mine a hollow cross-course ran
From north to south, an omen of much good;
And tin lay heaped on stulls and level-plots;
And in each nook a tallow taper flared,
Where pale men wasted with exhaustion huge.
Here holes exploded, and there mallets rang,
And rocks fell crashing, lifting the stiff hair
From time-worn brows, and noisy buckets roared
In echoing shafts; and through this gulf of gloom
A hollow murmur rushed for evermore.

Stephen MacKenna (1872-1934) was an Irish literary scholar, journalist, conversationalist and classical translator who made his home at a cottage at Reskadinnick. He was said to be one of the greatest writers of prose of his time.

JOURNALS AND LETTERS
of
STEPHEN MACKENNA

Coracle

Before that he moved in Irish literary and theatrical circles. He is mentioned in James Joyce's famous novel 'Ulysses'. After fighting on the Greek side in their war against Turkey in 1897 he became an enthusiast for the Greek language and translated the works of the neo-Platonic scholar Plotinius.

He lived at Reskadinnick enjoying nature, befriending birds and tending his apple trees. He explored widely in Cornwall and spent almost all of the rest of his life there, before dying in a hospital in London. His life is recorded in the reference given.

Later, in the same cottage, **W. John Burley** (1914-2002), most famous for the Wycliffe detective novels, lived with his wife and children.

Originally he worked in the gas industry. The author remembers visiting him, with the author's father, when he lived in the gas manager's house at Tuckingmill (abutting the Red River). They were both interested in Natural History, particularly that of the Red River valley. Later he moved with his family to the cottage at Reskadinnick and continued to study the natural history of the valley.

He then decided to go as a mature student to Oxford to read for a degree in Zoology. On graduating he became a master at Newquay Grammar School but also took up writing the Wycliffe novels. They were highly successful and he retired from school teaching to write full time. These novels are still serialised on television.

Reskadinnick House is a beautiful Georgian semi-manor house built by the mining engineer Joseph Vivian.

Reskadinnick House (2012). (Author)

It has been well restored. The author **Molly Vivian Hughes** (1886-1956) records her holidays spent there in '*A London Family: 1870-1900*'. This is regarded as a classic of biographical writing. She describes Reskadinnick as 'synonymous with Paradise'. She loved her holidays spent with her grandparents there and describes outings around the neighbouring area. She also wrote the book '*Vivians, A Family in Victorian Cornwall*'.

Frank Turk (1911-1986) lived most of his life in a cottage at Reskadinnick with his wife **Stella** who still lives there.

Natural history meeting in Red River valley (mid 1950s). (Author) Author, Frank Turk, Author's father (J.K.Williams), Stella Turk.

They were both experts in botany, zoology, entomology and natural history in general. Frank was a polymath. He was a very clever and deep intellectual who ventured into many fields. As well as natural history he studied Chinese and Japanese culture and religion, archaeology and art. Spending most of his life in the Red River valley he walked up and down it many times, observing it over time and, in particular, its natural history. His garden contained (and still does) a very wide range of plants, shrubs and sculptures, some from far away. He supported himself by becoming a WEA lecturer (he was formerly an external Reader at London University). As an exceptionally inspiring lecturer he enthused many others who were educated in his classes, in particular John Burley and the author's father.

Stella became an expert in molluscs, seashore life and woods. She has a large collection of specimens of these and has been the author of a number of books on shells including the widely read Foyle's handbook.

Frank and Stella were both enthusiasts for Siamese cats which they bred. They knew Harold Wilson who was also a Siamese cat enthusiast and they bred and boarded his cat, Nemo. Frank once remarked on the variety and number of literary figures who had been attracted to live in the valley and in particular Reskadinnick. Some of them are mentioned above.

REFERENCES AND BIBLIOGRAPHY

Listed below are publications which have been used in the preparation of this book together with other useful publications which treat some of the subject matter in greater depth.

Sharpe (1990) provides a very comprehensive description and list of the prehistoric and historic sites in the valley as well as their grid references.

A very different book is Southam, D.M. Thomas, Turk and Ruhrmund (1989), which is noteworthy for its excellent photographs of some of the sites and the river in states that no longer exist.

The sites at Gwithian/Godrevy are discussed in many papers particularly those by Charles Thomas. However most of this work has now been rewritten in Kirkham and Herring (eds) (2007) with contributions by Blackman, Ramsey, Cook, Hamilton, Marshall, Nowakowski, Quinnell, Roberts, Sturgess, Charles Thomas, Nicholas Thomas and Thorpe. Therefore, not all the original papers are referenced.

Trounson (1980) contains many historical photographs, mainly of the mines.

Thomas (1958) gives an account of St. Gothian's chapel and the history of Gwithian.

Childe (1951) and McGrail (1978) mention the logboat and adze found at Tuckingmill.

Symons lists all the tin streaming works in 1884.

Walker has done bore sampling in the lower reaches of the valley and come to the conclusion (contradicting previous assumptions) that the sea never came in further than just above Gwithian Bridge.

Other references are self-explanatory by their titles.

An Archaeological Assessment of The Camborne Waste Water Treatment Works in the Red River Valley, Cornwall Archaeological Unit, Cornwall County Council, 1996.

Buckley, A., Historical Evidence of Alluvial Tin Streaming in the River Valleys of Camborne, Illogan and Redruth, *Journal of the Trevithick Society*, **26**, 1999, 87-99.

Buckley, J.A., *The Cornish Mining Industry, a brief history*, Tor Mark Press, Redruth, 2002.

Bullen, L.J., *Mining in Cornwall: Camborne to Redruth*, Volume 8 (2013), The Historic Press, Stroud.

Childe, V.G., Exotic Stone Adze from Tuckingmill, Camborne, Cornwall, *Proceedings of the Prehistoric Society*, **17; 96** (1951).

Darling, A., W.J. Burley, 1914-2002: Zoologist, Teacher, Writer, *Journal of the Royal Institution of Cornwall*, 2013, 117-134.

Dodds, E.R. (Ed), *Journal and Letters of Stephen MacKenna*, Constable, London 1936.

Everett, D., (ed.) *The Cornish Poet: poems of John Harris (1820 - 1884);* Loughborough: Zipped Books 2002.

Fowler, P.J. A Native Homestead of the Roman Period at Porth Godrevy, Gwithian, *Cornish Archaeology* No. 1 (1962) 17-60.

Hughes, M.V., *Vivians A Family in Victorian Cornwall*, Oxford University Press, Oxford, 1984.

Hughes, M.V., *A London Family 1870-1900,* Oxford University Press, Oxford, 1991.

Jackson, B. & E. Wildlife in the Red RiverValley (includes a list of species), Unpublished MS. 2011.

Kirkham, G. *Gwithian Streamworks,* Cornwall Archaeological Unit, Report No. 2005R029, 2005.

Kirkham, G., and P. Herring, *Cornish Archaeology* (A special edition revisiting the archaeological excavations at Gwithian), **46** (2007).

Lee, G.S. Prospecting for Tin in the Sands of St. Ives Bay, Cornwall, *Min. Ind. (Trans. Inst. Min. Metall A),* **77** (1968) A49-A64.

McGrail, S., *Logboats of England and Wales Part 1,* B.A.R. Oxford, 1978.

Mitchell, J. and S. Moore, *Tuckingmill Valley Park Management Plan,* Kerrier District Council, Helston, 2009.

Nowakowski, J.A., Life and Death in a Cornish Valley, *British Archaeology* **89** (July-August 2007), 13-17.

O'Neil, B.H. St. J., The Roman Villa at Magor Farm, near Camborne, Cornwall, *Journal of the Royal Institution of Cornwall,* **24, 1-2**, appendix volume 1, (1934),1-59.

Red River Valley Local Nature Reserve leaflet:

http://cornwallmaps.org/cms/camborne/things-to-do-in-camborne/nature-reserves/red-river-valley-lnr

Sharpe, A., *The Red River Trail, An Archaeological Assessment,* Cornwall Archaeological Unit, Cornwall County Council, Truro, 1990.

Southam, J, Thomas, D.M, Turk, F. and J. Ruhrmund, *The Red River,* Cornerhouse Publications, Manchester, 1989.

Symons, R. *A Geographical Dictionary, or Gazatteer of the County of Cornwall,* F.Rodda, Penzance, 1884.

Tangye, M., Earthworks in the Parish of Illogan, *Cornish Archaeology,* **10** (1971), 37-48.

Tangye, M. Hulls in Cornwall: A Survey and Discussion, *Cornish Archaeology,* **12** (1973), 31-52.

Tangye, M., *Tehidy and the Bassets,* Truran, Redruth, 1984.

Thomas, C., Gwithian: Ten Years Work, *West Cornwall Field Club,* Camborne, 1958.

Thomas, C., *Gwithian,* P.R. Earle, Camborne, 1964.

Thomas, C., Minor Sites in the Gwithian Area, *Cornish Archaeology,* No. 3 (1964) 37-62.

Thomas, C., Roman Objects from the Gwithian Area, *Cornish Archaeology,* **11** (1972) 53-55.

Thomas, C., and J. Mann, *Godrevy Light,* Twelveheads Publications, Chacewater, Truro 2009.

Trounson, J.H., *Mining in Cornwall, 1850-1960,* Vols. I and II, Moorland Publishing, Nottingham, 1980.

Tuckingmill Valley Park leaflet:

https://www.cornwall.gov.uk/media/3620347/Tuckingmill-VP-MAP.pdf

https://www.cornwall.gov.uk/media/3620348/Tuckingmill-VP-leaflet-front-cover.pdf

Walker, T.M. *Shifting Sand; the Palaeoenvironment and Archaeology of Blown Sand in Cornwall.* Unpublished PhD thesis, University of Reading, 2014.

INDEX

Arsenic, 12, 40, 41, 55
Arsenic Flues, 12, 42, 46, 59
Arsenic Stacks, 12

Bal Maidens, 1, 37
Barripper, 14
Basset family, 12, 34, 76
Beam Engines, 1, 35
Beeble River, 14
Bell Lake, 13, 53, 54, 59, 61
Blackman, Tony, 73
Bolenowe, 7, 8, 9, 10, 21, 59, 63, 83
Bolenowe Carn Moor, 20, 21
Boswyn, 14
Brea, 9, 11, 22, 37, 38, 59
Brea Adit, 11, 36
Bronze, 7, 24
Bronze Age, 7, 20, 23, 28, 29
Buckley, Allen, 74
Burley, W. John, 68, 71, 74
Buddles, 1, 36, 37, 47
Bullen, L.J. 74

Calciners, 40, 55
Camborne, 2, 12, 18
Camborne-Redruth Bypass, 2, 12, 57, 58
Canalisation of river, 12, 14, 60
Carlenno Round, 27
Carn Brea, 22, 35
Carwynnen Quoit, 14
Ceres Rock, 30
Childe, V.G., 73, 74
Cober River, 8
Cook, Gordon, 73
Cook's Kitchen Mine, 35

Connor River, 14, 15
Connerton, 32
Coombe, 12, 52, 53, 59
Copper, 7, 34, 64, 65, 83
Crane Godrevy, 27, 32, 33
Crowan Beacon, 21
Courtyard Houses, 21, 22

Dark Ages, 20, 29, 30, 33
Darling, Andrew, 74
Dodds, E.R, 74
Dolcoath Mine, 2, 35, 63
Domesday Book, 32
Dumnonii Tribe, 27

East Pool Mine, 35
Engine Houses, 66, 67
Everett, D, 74

Forest, 8
Fougous, 22
Fowler, P.J, 74

Garrack, 28, 32
Godrevy, 9, 16, 19, 24, 27, 29, 30, 33, 48, 55, 73, 74, 76
Gwealavellan, 32
Gwithian, 9, 14, 15, 16, 22, 29, 30, 32, 54, 60, 73, 74, 75, 76, 84

Hamilton, Derek, 73
Hangman's Barrow, 20
Harris, John, 63, 74
Hayle River, 8
Hell's Mouth, 14
Helston, 8, 24
Herring, Peter, 73, 75
Hughes, Molly, 70, 74, 75
Hulls, 22, 76

Indium, 6, 60
Iron Age, 7, 20, 21, 22, 24, 27, 28, 32

Jackson, Brian, 75
Jackson, Elizabeth, 61, 75
James Tables, see Vibrating Tables

Kieve Mill, 12, 48, 49, 50, 51, 52, 59
Kirkham, Graeme, 75

Lee, G.S, 75
Logboats, 23, 24, 73, 75
Loe Pool, 8

McGrail, S, 73, 75
MacKenna, Stephen, 67, 74
Magor Round, 27
Magor Villa, 26, 29
Mann, Jessica, 19, 76
Marram Grass, 29, 30
Marshall, Peter, 73
Medieval Period, 32, 33
Menadarva, 14, 27, 29, 31, 33, 54, 59, 61
Mesolithic Period, 28
Mitchell, J, 75
Moore, S, 75
Mount Whistle Round, 25

Nanterrow, 27
Neolithic Period, 22
Newton Moor, 9, 59, 83
North Crofty Mine, 35
Nowakowski, Jacqueline A, 73, 75

O'Neil, B.H. St, 75

Pendarves Manor, 14
Pennance Round, 27
Peter, Thurstan, 24
Pool, 12
Porth Godrevy, 28, 29, 74
Praze-an-Beeble, 14
Ponsprittal, 14, 59

Quinnell, Henrietta, 73

Rag Frames, 1, 3, 37, 47, 50
Ramsey, Christopher, Bronk, 73
Red River Nature Reserve, 59, 75
Reskadinnick, 12, 47, 48, 59, 67, 68, 70, 71, 72, 83
Reskadinnick House, 12, 69
Reskajeage, 14, 15, 18, 27, 28, 32
Redruth, 18, 83
Roberts, Helen, 73
Roman (Romano-British) Period, 7, 21, 26, 28, 29, 74
Roscroggan, 5, 6, 12, 25, 47, 59, 60, 61
Rosewarne Manor, 12
Roseworthy, 14
Roskear, 24, 57
Ruhrmund, Jan, 73, 76

St. Derwa's Chapel, 31
St. Gothians Chapel, 30
Settling Beds, 11, 37, 38, 39, 51
Sharpe, Adam, 73, 75
South Crofty Mine, 5, 6, 35, 57, 58, 60
Southam, Jem, 10, 15, 39, 40, 73, 76
Stamps, 1, 35, 36, 37
Sturgess, Joanna, 73
Symons, J.R, 73, 76

Tangye, Michael, 76
Tehidy, 12, 34
Tehidy House, 12
Tehidy Stream, 12, 13, 27, 52, 59
Thomas, Charles, 19, 73, 76
Thomas, D.M, 73, 76
Thomas, Nicholas, 73
Thorpe, Carl, 73
Tin, 1, 6, 7, 11, 12, 13, 17, 19, 21, 22, 28, 32, 33, 34, 37, 40, 45, 47, 48, 49, 55, 56, 57, 59, 60, 61, 73, 74, 75
Tincroft Mine, 35
Tin Smelting, 30, 40

Tolgarrick Tin Streaming Works, 40
Tolvaddon, 12, 24, 40, 42, 43, 44, 45, 46, 57, 58, 59
Trevoryan Round, 27
Trounson, J.H, 73, 76
Truro Museum, 24, 25
Tuckingmill, 2, 3, 4, 12, 23, 24, 33, 34, 36, 38, 39, 59, 68, 73, 74, 75
Tuckingmill Valley Park, 12, 57, 59, 61, 76
Turk, Frank, 71, 73, 76
Turk, Stella, 71

Vibrating Tables, 37
Vivian, Joseph, 69

Walker, Tom, 74, 77
Water Wheels, 33, 36
West Seton Mine, 35, 46, 47
Western United Mines, 5
Wheal Agar Mine, 35
Wheal Grenville Mine, 35
Woolf, Virginia, 19

Zinc, 6, 60

THE AUTHOR

Professor H. Paul Williams was born in Redruth and spent all his childhood in a house above the Tehidy stream, a tributary of the Red River, with tin streaming of its own and less than a mile from the main river. All his traceable ancestors on his father's side lived their lives close to the Red River at Bolenowe, Newton Moor, Treskillard, Condurrow and Beacon. Most of the men were tin or copper miners. His Great Grandfather was a cooper and worked the compressor at Dolcoath mine. His Great Grandmother was a tin streamer and his Grandfather and Grandmother were employed respectively at the mining service companies of Holmans (making mining equipment) and Bickford Smiths (making fuses for explosives for the mines). They lived for much of their retirement at Redlands, an attractive house in the Red River valley.

Redlands in the River Valley near Reskadinnick (2012).   (Author)

Paul Williams spent much of his childhood playing in the Red River valley and the Tehidy tributary, climbing through the deserted arsenic flues, wading through the river and cycling along now overgrown paths. He attended Pool Infants, Barncoose

Primary and Redruth Grammar School. During the 1950s he participated in the dig of prehistoric sites at Gwithian. He went to Cambridge University where he read Mathematics. Vacation jobs were taken working for Holmans and working on a tin dredger prospecting for tin in St. Ives Bay. Then he completed a PhD in Mathematical Logic at Leicester University before working in Industry and Academia, latterly as a Professor at The London School of Economics, where he is now Emeritus Professor. Professor Williams has had a house in Cornwall, near Helston, for most of his adult life. He still spends time exploring and walking the Red River Valley. He is a member of the Royal Institution of Cornwall and the Cornwall Archaeological Society.

Made in the USA
Columbia, SC
27 August 2018